Lerner SPORTS

SPORTS ALL-STARS

LEBRON JAMES

2ND EDITION

Jon M. Fishman

D1088532

Lerner Publications ◆ Minneapolis

Lerner Publications Company
An imprint of Lerner Publishing Group, Inc.
241 First Avenue North
Minneapolis, MN 55401 USA

For reading levels and more information, look up this title at www.lernerbooks.com.

Main body text set in Albany Std. Typeface provided by Agfa.

Library of Congress Cataloging-in-Publication Data

Names: Fishman, Jon M., author.
Title: Lebron James / Jon M. Fishman.
Description: Second edition. | Minneapolis, MN : Lerner Publications, [2021] | Series: Sports all-stars (Lerner sports) | Includes bibliographical references and index. | Audience: Ages 7–11 | Audience: Grades 2–3 | Summary: "LeBron James of the Los Angeles Lakers has wowed basketball fans throughout his career. Dig deeper into James's impressive play, discover how he stays on top, and learn more about his life outside of basketball"— Provided by publisher.
Identifiers: LCCN 2020039123 (print) | LCCN 2020039124 (ebook) | ISBN 9781728404363 (library binding) | ISBN 9781728423173 (paperback) | ISBN 9781728418827 (ebook other)
Subjects: LCSH: James, LeBron—Juvenile literature. | Basketball players—United States—Biography—Juvenile literature. | African American basketball players—Biography—Juvenile literature.
Classification: LCC GV884.J36 F57 2021 (print) | LCC GV884.J36 (ebook) | DDC 796.323092 [B]—dc23

LC record available at https://lccn.loc.gov/2020039123
LC ebook record available at https://lccn.loc.gov/2020039124

Manufactured in the United States of America
1-48494-49008-10/2/2020

TABLE OF CONTENTS

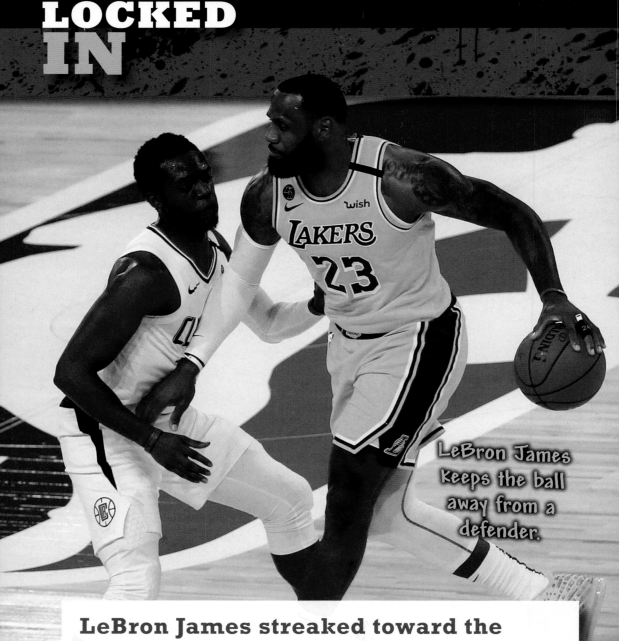

LeBron James keeps the ball away from a defender.

LeBron James streaked toward the basket. Los Angeles Clippers defenders tried to stop him, but they couldn't even slow him down. James scored to give the Los Angeles Lakers a 101–98 lead.

FACTS
AT A GLANCE

- **Date of Birth:** December 30, 1984

- **Position:** forward and guard

- **League:** National Basketball Association (NBA)

- **Professional Highlights:** played in the NBA Finals eight years in a row; won four NBA championships; played in 16 NBA All-Star Games

- **Personal Highlights:** grew up in Akron, Ohio; supports kids through the LeBron James Family Foundation; appeared in the movies *Trainwreck* and *Space Jam: A New Legacy*

James and his teammates were playing for the first time in more than four months. Beginning on March 12, 2020, the National Basketball Association (NBA) shut down in the middle of the season. The day before, a player had tested positive for the disease COVID-19. To prevent the disease from spreading, the league suspended all games.

James dunks the ball for two points.

The NBA returned to action on July 30. To avoid travel that might expose players and others to COVID-19, teams played at Walt Disney World in Orlando, Florida. Players would stay there until the end of the season. James vowed to play his best. "I'll be as locked in as I can be under the circumstances," he said.

James was locked in against the Clippers. After his basket gave the Lakers a three-point lead, the Clippers tied the score 101–101. With less than 20 seconds left in the game, James drove to the basket again. This time, Clippers defenders blocked his path. James put up a shot, but the ball bounced off the front of the basket.

James, surrounded by Clippers defenders, scores the winning basket for the Lakers.

James didn't give up. He jumped toward the basket and grabbed the ball. Before his feet touched the court, he shot again and scored. The Lakers won the game 103–101. The win helped Los Angeles hold onto the best record in the Western Conference. James and his teammates were determined to win the NBA championship.

James signs copies of his book at a bookstore in Ohio.

"I first started playing basketball when I was about 9 [years old]," James wrote in a book about his childhood. Before that he played football. He liked football because he could score touchdowns. He was still too short to dunk a basketball.

LeBron jumps for a dunk during a St. Vincent-St. Mary High School basketball game.

It didn't take LeBron long to grow into basketball. He was tall and strong by the time he reached St. Vincent-St. Mary (SVSM) High School in Akron, Ohio. From there, his basketball career took off like a rocket. As a freshman in 1999–2000, he averaged 21 points per game. The team lost just once all year and won the state title.

The team won the state championship again in 2000–2001. LeBron was even better than he had been the year before. Fans and scouts around the country were taking notice. He appeared on the February 18, 2002, cover of *Sports Illustrated*. The headline read, "The Chosen One."

The honors and big games kept coming. He scored 50 points in one game. Then he scored 52 points in a game SVSM won, 78–52. LeBron scored as many points alone as the opposing team scored total! He averaged more than 30 points per game as a senior in 2002–2003. For the third time since he joined the school, SVSM won the state title.

In 2003, he was named Gatorade Player of the Year for the second time. The award is given to the best high school athlete in a sport in the United States. LeBron was the first person to ever win the award twice.

LeBron takes the ball down the court during a 2003 SVSM game.

LeBron poses for a photo after winning the 2003 Gatorade Player of the Year award.

2003 NATIONAL BOYS BASKETBALL PLAYER LEBRON JAMES

LeBron holds up his Cleveland jersey
after joining the team in 2003.

Scouts thought LeBron was *by far* the best basketball recruit in the country. Some were calling him the best young player since the great Michael Jordan. Most players go to college for at least a year before playing in the NBA. But LeBron chose to skip college. The Cleveland Cavaliers chose him with the first pick in the 2003 NBA Draft. "I'm staying in Cleveland, and I'm real excited," LeBron said.

James runs down the court during a game.

James can run faster than most players his size. He jumps higher and stays in the air longer. He can spin and turn more quickly. Natural talent is a big part of his success. But James also works *really* hard to keep his body in top shape.

During the NBA season, James exercises every day. Games and practices keep him busy from fall until spring. He works out a lot during the offseason too: five to seven days a week. If you stop by his house in the morning, don't worry about waking James up. He often rises at 5 a.m. to begin his workouts.

James warms up before a game.

A normal day begins with icing and stretching his muscles to keep them loose and prevent injury. He also does yoga to strengthen and stretch his muscles. After that, James may head to the gym to lift weights. On other days, he goes to the basketball court. He shoots, dribbles, and practices all the skills he needs during games.

James ices his knees

James often wears high-tech gear when he works out. The devices check his heart rate. They keep track of how far he runs and how many calories he burns.

James drinks a sports drink during warm-ups.

Some athletes eat huge amounts of food to keep from getting too skinny. James doesn't eat much more than most people. He starts each morning with two big glasses of water. He likes chicken breasts—without the skin. Pasta, fruit, vegetables, and other healthful foods are also on his menu. He treats himself with pie, pizza, and french fries but never before a game.

With 82 games in the NBA season, James gets sore and tired. He drinks a special mixture after games to help him recover water he lost sweating on the court. The mixture contains water and carbohydrates (carbs) his body needs to recover. Then he sinks to the waist in an icy bath. The ice helps his muscles feel less sore the next day.

If the game was in another city, James and his teammates usually hop on an airplane after leaving the arena. Even in the air, James continues working on his body to get ready for the next day. He receives a massage and wears special clothing to get his blood flowing. Electronic devices make his muscles twitch to keep them loose. A careful postgame diet with lots of carbs flushes toxins from his body. His career depends on his body, and James works hard to keep it running.

THE KING

James appeared on *Good Morning America* in 2016.

James is surrounded by cameras as he runs onto the court for a 2020 game in Los Angeles.

LeBron James is one of the rare athletes who fans know instantly by just his first name. He's the top player in the NBA and a worldwide sports celebrity. In recent years, his star power has surged way beyond the basketball court.

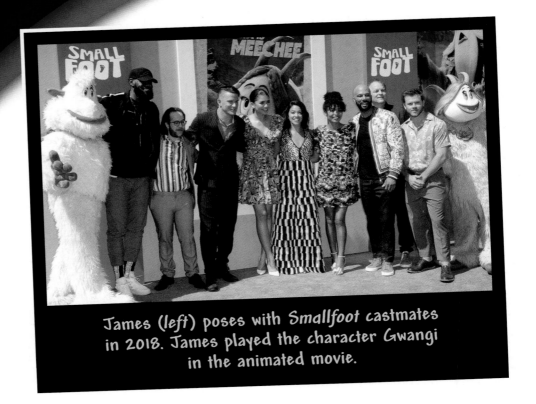

James (left) poses with *Smallfoot* castmates in 2018. James played the character Gwangi in the animated movie.

King James, as he's known to fans, can often be seen on TV. And not just during Cavs games. James has appeared on TV shows from *Good Morning America* to *The Tonight Show Starring Jimmy Fallon*. He hosted *Saturday Night Live*. He even voiced himself on an episode of *The Simpsons*.

He's been popping up on the big screen lately too. Older audiences thought he was really funny when he played himself in the 2015 movie *Trainwreck*. Some critics even said he stole the show. Fans of all ages will look for him in the upcoming movie *Space Jam: A New Legacy*.

More Than a Vote

James uses his status as a world-famous athlete to promote social justice. He talks publicly about the unjust killings of Black people and other people of color by police officers. He supports athletes who follow Colin Kaepernick's lead by kneeling during the US national anthem to protest this violence

In 2020, James and other athletes and entertainers started More Than a Vote. The group encourages Black people and other people of color to vote by providing help and information about voting. "We feel like we're getting some ears and some attention, and this is the time for us to finally make a difference," James said.

Colin Kaepernick (center, right) and San Francisco 49ers teammate Eric Reid kneel during the US national anthem in 2016.

Companies are eager to work with James. He has helped sell products for Coca-Cola, Dunkin, and many others. In 2015, he agreed to a lifetime deal to represent Nike. It was the first time the company had agreed to such a long deal with an athlete.

With money from the NBA, Nike, and others, James is rich. In 2019–2020, he earned $88.2 million. That made him the fifth-highest-paid athlete in the world.

James spent some of that money on a six-bedroom home in Akron. The house has a huge game room and plenty of space for his family. In 2013, James and Savannah Brinson got married. The couple began dating when they were both in high school. They have three children: LeBron Jr., Bryce, and Zhuri. LeBron Jr. is already a force on the basketball court as a teenager.

James ties his Nikes on the court.

James poses with kids at a LeBron James Family Foundation event.

There are rumors that some college teams have already offered him a place on their teams.

James is closely connected to his community. He uses his star power and money to make Ohio a better place. The LeBron James Family Foundation works to strengthen communities and promote education. The foundation helps more than 1,400 students in the Akron area. It provides scholarships, support programs, and mentors to help kids succeed in school.

LEGEND

James helps the Cavs beat the Detroit Pistons in 2005.

The 2002–2003 Cleveland Cavaliers were tied for the worst record in the NBA at 17–65. Then they drafted James. The 2003–2004 Cleveland Cavaliers were better. They ended the season 35–47. James was voted Rookie of the Year.

Could James play in the National Football League (NFL)? Since he played football as a child, many people would like to find out. Rumors of him returning to the sport have always followed him. In 2015, James put the rumors to rest and said he wouldn't play in the NFL. "Love it still though," he wrote on Twitter.

The Cavs got better each year with James. In 2006–2007, he helped the team reach the NBA Finals. But the San Antonio Spurs beat them in four games.

After the 2009–2010 season, James announced he was leaving Cleveland. The news crushed Cavs fans. He joined a group of stars on the Miami Heat. James, Dwyane Wade, and Chris Bosh were a mighty force on the court. The Heat won the NBA championship in 2011–2012 and 2012–2013. With two titles, James had reached the peak as an NBA player.

James holds the Finals Most Valuable Player Award with his right hand and the NBA championship trophy with his left after winning the title in 2016.

King James returned to Cleveland for 2014–2015. When he and the Cavs won the NBA title in 2016, his place as a basketball legend was secure. Cleveland made the NBA Finals in 2017 and 2018, but they lost both series to the Golden State Warriors. Between Miami and

Cleveland, James played in the Finals an incredible eight years in a row.

In 2018–2019, James moved again and joined the Lakers. His Finals streak ended that season. But with fellow superstar Anthony Davis, James led Los Angeles to the Finals in 2019–2020. They beat Miami in six games to claim the title. James became NBA champion for the fourth time, and he won his fourth Finals Most Valuable Player Award.

James has played in 16 NBA All-Star Games and has won the NBA Most Valuable Player Award four times. After almost 20 seasons, James is one of the oldest players in the league. But his reign as the king of the NBA will probably continue for years.

James played for Team USA at the 2004 Olympic Games in Athens, Greece. The team finished third, but James and his teammates won gold in 2008 and 2012.

All-Star Stats

James turned 35 during the 2019–2020 season. He ranks high on the NBA's all-time points list. Yet many NBA stars play into their late 30s. Look at how James compares to some of the league's greatest players ever. By the time he retires, he could rank even higher on this list.

Most Career Points Scored by an NBA Player*

Player	Points
Kareem Abdul-Jabbar	38,387
Karl Malone	36,928
LeBron James	34,241
Kobe Bryant	33,643
Michael Jordan	32,292
Dirk Nowitzki	31,560
Wilt Chamberlain	31,419
Julius Irving	30,026
Moses Malone	29,580
Shaquille O'Neal	28,596

*Through the 2019–2020 season

Glossary

calories: units of energy

carbohydrates: substances in food that the body needs for energy

critics: people who judge art such as films and books

draft: a yearly event in which teams take turns choosing players

dunk: to throw the ball through the basket with the hands above the rim

mentor: a trusted teacher or guide

recruit: a player who is being considered for the next level

rookie: a first-year player

scholarships: money given to students to help them pay for school

scouts: people who judge the skills of basketball players

toxins: poisons

yoga: exercise that includes careful breathing and body control

6   Associated Press, "Things to Know about the NBA
    Season Restart Tonight," *Chicago Sun-Times*, July 30,
    2020, https://chicago.suntimes.com/2020/7/30/21348151
    /nba-restart-things-to-know.

8   Buzz Bissinger and LeBron James. *LeBron's Dream
    Team: How Four Friends and I Brought a Championship
    Home* (New York: Penguin Books, 2010), 17.

12 Tom Canavan, "Cavaliers Win LeBron James Sweepstakes,"
    Pittsburgh Post-Gazette, May 23, 2003, http://old.post
    -gazette.com/sports/other/20030523cavsjamesso6.asp.

21 Jonathan Martin, "LeBron James and other Stars Form
    a Voting Rights Group," *New York Times*, last modified
    July 18, 2020, https://www.nytimes.com/2020/06/10/us
    /politics/lebron-james-voting-rights.html.

25 Micah Peters, "The 10 Most Interesting Parts of LeBron
    James' Twitter Q&A," *USA Today*, July 28, 2015, http://
    ftw.usatoday.com/2015/07/10-most-interesting-parts-of
    -lebron-james-twitter-qa.

Learn More

The LeBron James Family Foundation
https://www.lebronjamesfamilyfoundation.org

LeBron James Stats
https://www.basketball-reference.com/players/j/jamesle01.html

Levit, Joe. *Basketball's G.O.A.T. Michael Jordan, LeBron James, and More*. Minneapolis: Lerner Publications, 2020.

Los Angeles Lakers
https://www.nba.com/lakers/

Scheff, Matt. *NBA and WNBA Finals: Basketball's Biggest Playoffs*. Minneapolis: Lerner Publications, 2021.

Wetzel, Dan. *Epic Athletes: LeBron James*. New York: Henry Holt, 2019.

Index

Photo Acknowledgments

Image credits: Mike Ehrmann/Pool Photo via AP, pp. 4, 6, 7; AP Photo/Amy Sancetta, p. 8; AP Photo/Bruce Schwartzman, pp. 9, 10; AP Photo/Greg Ruffing, p. 11; AP Photo/Tony Dejak, p. 12; AP Photo/Chuck Burton, p. 13; AP Photo/Marcio Jose Sanchez, pp. 14, 21, 22; AP Photo/Wilfredo Lee, pp. 15, 16; Steven Ferdman/Everett Collection/Alamy Stock Photo, p. 18; AP Photo/Kelvin Kuo, p. 19; Sthanlee B. Mirador/Sipa via AP Images, p. 20; AP Photo/Alex Menendez, p. 23; Icon Sports Media 441/Newscom, p. 24; AP Photo/Eric Risberg, p. 26.

Cover: Stacy Revere/Getty Images.